NORTHERN

RENAISSANCE

Series Editor: Wendy Shore
Written by: David Gillerman

© 1980 Woodbine Books, Inc.

ISBN 0-934516-12-X (series)
0-934516-01-4 (volume)
Manufactured in U.S.A.

Created by Shorewood Fine Art Books, New York,
for Woodbine Books, Inc.

THE COLLECTIONS

PIETER BRUEGHEL THE ELDER

Pieter Brueghel the Elder (ca. 1525–1569) is thought to have been born either in Breda, north of Antwerp, or in Brögel, in Belgian Limburg. A contemporary biographer, Karel van Mander, informs us that he studied with Pieter Cocke in Brussels. In 1551 Brueghel became a master in the Antwerp guild, and shortly thereafter he began a trip through France to Italy. He arrived in Rome in 1553 and seems to have travelled as far south as Sicily. He returned through the Alps, and by 1554 he was at work as an engraver for the Antwerp publisher Hieronymus Cock. Brueghel was deeply affected by the fierce social conflicts of his troubled period. Throughout his career he preferred satirical subjects drawn from folklore or the daily life of common people; however, where his early works are gay and gentle mockeries of human foibles, his later works are bitter and harsh, despairing of humanity's ability to rise above impoverishment and strife. In 1563 Brugehel married and moved to Brussels, where he remained until his death.

The Harvesters (1565)
By the mid-sixteenth century, Netherlandish painters could no longer claim to be the leaders of the Northern Renaissance. In fact, it would have been difficult for the painters of any national school to justifiably make that claim, because by that time all the most important properties of Renaissance art, in both its northern and Italian variants, were largely shared qualities. The court portraitists had already coined an international language by the beginning of the century, and by the century's midpoint, masters of narrative painting were fast catching up. For example, in Antwerp, where Pieter Brueghel began his professional career, the most popular artist of the day was one Frans Floris, who had made an aesthetic pilgrimage to Rome and whose paintings then became filled with ostentatious references to the most modern Italian works. Brueghel himself had made a long sojourn in Italy, but seems to have been more impressed by the country's landscape than by its art, and, unlike many of his contemporaries, formed a style which made no significant concession to Italian art. However, Brueghel does not seem to have suffered the alienation of a nonconformist; in Brussels, where he spent his last and most productive years, he is known to have received important public and private commissions. This painting, which is one of a series illustrating the months of the year, was bought and probably commissioned by Niclaes Jonghelinck, to decorate his large Antwerp residence. Like the four other surviving members of the series, this painting, which probably represents August, shows the month's characteristic activity performed by small, anonymous figures and set in a vast landscape. As in Albrecht Altdorfer's landscape, our view is from a high vantage point, so that we see the small figures slightly from above. However, unlike that of Altdorfer, Brueghel's horizon is quite high, so that nowhere does a human head break the line of the horizon, and the soil becomes a background against which the figures mass together in a small corner of the picture's endless expanse.

CONTENTS

INTRODUCTION

In looking back on the history of European civilization from the vantage point of his own century, the British philosopher Francis Bacon (1561–1626) chose gunpowder, the compass, and the printing press as the symbols of the most important fields of human endeavor. The first of these, symbolizing imperialistic conquest, was an invention of the middle ages, but during the Renaissance centuries we often observe the even more predominant influence of marriage in the shaping of national boundaries. For example, the marriage in 1496 of Philip I, the future Holy Roman Emperor, to Joanna, daughter of Ferdinand and Isabella of Spain, yielded a domain stretching from Gibraltar to the shores of the Baltic.

The compass, though also known in medieval times, is more appropriately the symbol of the fifteenth and sixteenth centuries, an age of global exploration and discovery. The Italian Christopher Columbus stands as the greatest hero of the period, but with the shift of power from a weakening, strife-torn Italy to the seafaring Atlantic states of England, France, Spain and the Netherlands, it was to be the northerners who reaped the material rewards of the New World.

The invention of the printing press, finally, belongs exclusively to the Northern Renaissance, and symbolizes the growing literacy and the spread of learning which marked that era. The invention of movable type by Johannes Gutenberg in 1456 was soon followed by the appearance of printing in all the major capitals, and with it the growth of humanism—*humanitas* being the Latin word for "literary activity"—a phenomenon stressing the worldly and intellectual achievements of man. The growth in literary activity and the resulting increase in the numbers of both books and readers created a new literary freedom and, therefore, diversity of opinion. The advent of printing also had its effect on the age of exploration and its inevitable consequences. If, as a result of the discovery of a new continent, the population of Europe would slowly disperse itself across another hemisphere, now even the most remote outpost would be linked to the homeland by this new means of mass communication. The territorialism and parochialism born of feudal society were finally dying.

In its place came capitalism—a system of free enterprise, as people formerly bound to the land and required to pay taxes or tithes to their feudal lords could now move to the towns, whose rapid growth welcomed new populations and gave rise to a strong middle class.

The feudal society of the middle ages was the last to die in the territory of Burgundy, which, for the history of northern art in the fifteenth and sixteenth centuries, was a region of the utmost importance. Consisting of present-day Belgium, parts of Holland—collectively called the Netherlands in those times—and parts of northern and northeastern France, Burgundy was ruled by a succession of powerful dukes and was one of the last feudal strongholds to surrender its independence to a monarchic power. (This occurred in 1486, when it was annexed by the Holy Roman Empire.) Each of

Burgundy's major cities, Bruges, Ghent, and Antwerp, was a thriving commercial center, and each in turn was the home of its own school of painting.

The painters of these cities could not boast an artistic independence to equal their political autonomy—not before the early years of the fifteenth century, at any rate. Before about 1420 they had largely relied on the French for their ideas, though not even the artists of Paris could claim to possess a totally individual style. At the end of the fourteenth and into the beginning of the fifteenth century, a mode now known as the International Style was favored by almost all of the regional schools of European painters. This style chose the illuminated book as its favorite medium, and offered a reflection of the courtly life of princes and monarchs across the continent. The break-down of its careful avoidance of natural appearances only began after 1400, largely through the efforts of Burgundian painters working in France. The expansion of its minute scale was never attempted before the appearance of the Master of Flémalle, the first artist of the Northern Renaissance, whose style is marked by monumentality, naturalism, and dramatic presentation.

In addition to breaking a Europewide dependence on the International Style, important technical considerations also distinguish the Master of Flémalle from his predecessors. In contrast to the practitioners of the International Style, who were limited by their use of egg-based pigments known as tempera, the Master of Flémalle and his contemporaries used oil-based colors, and instead of applying these to paper they painted on separate wooden panels. The resulting works were inherently far more physically imposing than illuminated books, and the new procedure, which permanently changed the craft of painting, was an invaluable legacy to all subsequent European artists.

Yet there is little other than this similarity of technique to prepare us for the sudden leap forward taken by Jan van Eyck. Nor were his contemporaries quite prepared for the still greater realism and the increased drama of his new style. His fame spread throughout Europe and already in 1456 the Italian humanist Bartholomeo Fazio called him "the leading painter of our time." Roger van der Weyden, almost certainly the pupil of the Master of Flémalle, gleaned similar, if not quite equal, honors from the Italian. By 1449 Cyriaco d'Ancona, another Italian connoisseur, described a lost painting by Roger this way: "There you could see faces come alive and breathe which [Roger] wanted to show as living and likewise the deceased as dead, and in particular many garments...blooming meadows, flowers, trees...and everything else you would think to have been produced not by the artifice of human hands but by all-bearing nature itself." (*Northern Renaissance Art, 1400-1600, Sources and Documents,* Wolfgang Stechow, ed., Englewood Cliffs, N.J., 1966.) These same qualities, which are perhaps even more Jan van Eyck's than Roger van der Weyden's, still amaze us today, just as they amazed the Italians of the Renaissance.

Shortly before the beginning of the sixteenth century, the painters of Italy joined these art connoisseurs in their praise of the northerners, and exchanges between north and south soon followed. This was mainly due to the increasing mobility of artists, and to the dissemination of artists' prints. Probably the most widely travelled artist of his day was Albrecht Dürer, although he remained a lifelong resident of Nuremberg, his birthplace. On the other hand, artists such as Lucas Cranach and Hans Holbein the Younger, both of whom founded their careers on the portrayal of Europe's rich, royal, and noteworthy, could almost be described as itinerant and international, as their profession naturally demanded. In fact, as the sixteenth century progresses, relatively isolated and stationary figures, such as Albrecht Altdorfer and Matthias Grünewald, become increasingly rare. The pages of the printed book, meanwhile, provided a means of vicarious travel even for the like of Hieronymus Bosch, a Dutchman who seems to have rarely ventured outside his native village. His attachment to works which were available in facsimile, especially artists' prints and emblem books, explains the often uncanny similarities to his paintings that crop up in the works of the German artist Grünewald.

The most active role in the dissemination of printed art was played by Albrecht Dürer. Not only the publisher of his own prints, he was also a copyist and collector of other artists' prints, and during his last years devoted himself to the formulation of theories of art, these too promulgated through print.

"Printing was God's highest act of grace," Martin Luther proclaimed, and perhaps no other of the great giants of the Northern Renaissance owed more to it than he. Luther (1484-1546), the German religious reformer whose thought formed the basis of the Protestant Reformation, lived to see the wide and rapid spread of his ideas, whereas in former times they might have lain largely unknown between the leaves of a hand-written manuscript. Instead, by about 1525, Lutheranism, as his doctrines were then known, had found supporters and adherents in every stratum of northern society. Members of the artistic community, such as Lucas Cranach and Albrecht Dürer, were also converts, despite the dim view that some Lutherans took of religious painting. In the course of the later sixteenth century the Protestant north, as a result, was to see the maturation of other, previously less popular categories of painting, namely landscape, genre, still life and portraiture, and this, in turn, fostered a specialization on the part of the northern artist that was rare among his Italian counterparts.

In many parts of Europe, established Catholicism mounted stiff resistance to the Protestant advance, and this resulted in violent confrontations between members of opposing groups. The Counter-Reformation naturally originated in papal Rome, but it found its international support in the person of Emperor Charles V. His efforts to retard the Reformation, at first ambivalent, became more concentrated around the middle of the century, and eventually led to revolt in the former territories of Burgundy, dividing them into Protestant Holland in the North, and Catholic and Spanish Belgium in the South. Where sides had to be taken, political interests often overrode religious senti-ments. Francis I of France, though Catholic and the leader of a sophisticated, cultivated court where Italian influence prevailed in both religious and artistic matters, stood against Charles, and Henry VIII of England, though no Lutheran, opened the way to the Reformation in England by his split from the Roman Catholic Church and his self-appointment as head of the Church of England.

However, for most Europeans, not least for artists, Protestantism was more than just a cause over which to differ. Because Luther's writings condoned each Christian's embrace of a subjectively conceived God—no longer only the God of the Roman Catholic Church—and therefore the priesthood of all believers, they heralded, in the widest possible sense, the dawning of an age of individualism. It was an individualism that was fostered and encouraged by fortuitous timing—Luther's concept of God occurred at the same time as the advent of printing and the decline of feudalism. These three intertwined events contributed mightily to the decline of parochialism in Europe; the new climate allowed creative thinking in all areas of human endeavor. Thus, no weighing of merely material factors which contributed to, say, Pieter Brueghel's specialization in landscape and genre painting can complete our understanding of his truly transcendant individuality. And, in fact, this was a pronounced characteristic of all the greatest of his contemporaries.

MASTER OF FLEMALLE

The identity of the Master of Flémalle was once the subject of controversy; he has now been identified as Robert Campin (ca. 1378-1444). Campin is thought to have been born in Valenciennes; he later settled in Tournai, where he became a master in 1406 and a citizen in 1410. Numerous archival documents illuminate Campin's activities in Tournai, where he quickly rose to civic and professional eminence. By 1415 he was head of a large studio; in 1423 he became dean of the painters' guild and a member of the city council. Among the most innovative of the early Flemish artists, Campin broke with the Gothic International Style and chose instead a more naturalistic and poetic depiction of forms. Skilled in the use of light and shadow to model the faces and clothes of his subjects, Campin created an effect that was at once sweetly expressive and remarkably realistic. He died in Tournai.

The Annunciation (ca. 1427)

This painting is the center panel of a triptych and is called the Mérode Altarpiece, after its former owners. Not reproduced here are two flanking panels: the left-hand panel with the figures of the donors kneeling outside the Virgin's private chamber, and the right-hand panel with the figure of Joseph the carpenter, seated in his adjoining workroom, surrounded by the tools of his trade, and hard at work. The center panel includes a scene which at first strikes us as one of casual domestic life: there is little here, other than Gabriel's carefully smoothed and folded wings, to alert us to the impact of this winged visitor's intrusion. We look in on this meeting—as if through a window opposite the one in the back of the room—and our gaze travels from figure to figure and from the candlestick and lily atop the table, to the bench with its intricately carved figurines, to the fireplace and its screen, and to a bronze laver suspended within a niche. Everything has its place in this household, and the Master of Flémalle has been as painstaking in his recording of these objects as some discreet housekeeper has been in the arranging of them. However, the painter's exactitude is more than homage to a well-kept home. The laver and the lily were, to the knowing fifteenth-century viewer, familiar symbols of the eternal purity of the Mother of Christ. One might suppose that the Master of Flémalle, in his efforts to preserve the Virgin's domestic harmony, felt required to disguise these symbols of her celebrity. However, this fiction is not totally complete. Above the small bursts of glowing yellow light ignited by the undersides of the angel's wings, we can catch sight of an incongruously tiny white figure, bearing a matchstick cross and riding a beam of light on a path toward the Virgin. We can guess that this is the embryonic spirit of Christ, about to lodge itself in the womb of this serene woman. Elsewhere in the work the Master of Flémalle pursues his personal penchant for realistic detail; the broad smear of carbon climbing the back of the hearth and the nervous dash of gold around the Virgin's hem are just two such displays of this artist's great gift.

6

JAN VAN EYCK

Jan van Eyck (ca. 1390–1441) was probably born in Masseyck, in the Duchy of Limburg. By 1422 he was a painter in the court of John of Bavaria, Count of Holland, at The Hague; in 1425, upon the death of the Count, he was appointed court painter by Philip the Good, Duke of Burgundy. Beginning in 1426, Van Eyck undertook diplomatic missions for the Duke, travelling first to Spain and then to Portugal to participate in marriage negotiations. In 1430, he settled in Bruges. It is difficult to document Van Eyck's work; he left few signed pieces. Nevertheless, in works such as the famed *Ghent Altarpiece* (1426–32; Ghent, St. Bavon Cathedral), which he painted jointly with his brother Hubert, who died in 1426, Van Eyck reveals an innovative talent, forsaking the International Gothic style for a new sensibility. He combined a brilliant and fluid use of color with scrupulously realistic depiction of detail in both portraits and religious paintings. Van Eyck's technique set the standard for subsequent Flemish painting. He died in Bruges.

The Madonna of Chancellor Nicholas Rolin (ca. 1435)
As if in an impermeable turret, Madonna and Christ Child are seen sequestered in surroundings of a warm, glowing sumptuousness. Arcades with columns made of exotic stones, jasper, and porphyry, and crowned by figurated capitals, a floor with inlaid marble, and stained glass all intimate that these are exclusive quarters. Through the arches in the back of the room we have a view of a bustling city below, noticeably modern in its pointed architecture when compared to the hallowed age of the foreground interior. In the left side of the picture we see Nicholas Rolin (1376–1462), Philip the Good's chancellor of Burgundy and Brabant. He witnesses the coronation of the Mother and receives the benediction of the Child. The traditions of International style book illumination, from which Jan van Eyck emerged, had long condoned the temporary admission of mortals into the Virgin's sacred realm, provided they were accompanied by some sainted intercessor to act as advocate on their behalf, or provided they were represented in miniature, to denote their inferior status. However, by the time he came to paint this so-called "Madonna of Autun," Jan van Eyck had already developed an uncomprisingly realistic style. It was only by suggesting the otherworldiness of the chancellor's rendezvous, therefore, that he could avoid the patently fantastic formulae dictated by the work of his predecessors. All the interior's rare richness serves this very purpose. But although above and beyond the everyday world, this sanctum and its inhabitants are insistently real. Jan van Eyck counts every hair, every leaf, every bead, for each is pervaded by the spirit of which the Child Himself was but the physical embodiment. To have seen the supernatural in the real, and the real in the supernatural, made Jan van Eyck, at once, the greatest and the most characteristic artist of his time.

ROGER VAN DER WEYDEN

Roger van der Weyden (ca. 1399/1400–1464) was born in Tournai and worked in the shop of Robert Campin, the Master of Flémalle, from 1427 to 1432. By 1435 he had emigrated to Brussels, where he was named city painter. Roger made a pilgrimage to Italy in 1450, visiting Rome and Ferrara, where he was exposed to recent Italian developments in art and to new sources of patronage. Where Roger's earlier works are distinctive for their intensely mysterious quality and a sense of tragic beauty, brought about by a masterful use of chiaroscuro, his contact with the Italians softened and humanized his style considerably. Roger exerted a profound influence on his contemporaries and on many subsequent generations of European artists. Upon his return from Italy, Roger again settled in Brussels, where he worked until his death.

Mary Magdalen (ca. 1450–1452)

In the broad, triangular jaw and almond-shaped eyes of Roger van der Weyden's Magdalen, we detect a congenital likeness of the Mérode Virgin of the Master of Flémalle. This likeness is, in fact, our major justification for identifying the Master of Flémalle as one Robert Campin, an artist who signed no known works of art, but who is known to have been the teacher of Roger van der Weyden. Roger's five-year association with his teacher resulted in an intimate stylistic relationship between the two artists, particularly in their portrayals of women. Like the Mérode Virgin, Roger's Magdalen is pale-skinned and demure, her soft lips are slightly parted, and her lower lip casts a small shadow on her slightly pointed chin. The manual gestures of both women are carefully planned so as to occur against neutral backgrounds, creating a rhythmic dance of line across the picture surface. At the same time, this panel, which forms part of a triad known as the Triptych of Jean de Braque, reveals the strong impact that Jan van Eyck's painting had on Roger. The loving attention devoted to the intricately brocaded sleeve of the Magdalen's dress recalls the efforts of Jan van Eyck over similar details of texture. Even more important is Roger's pursuit of the sculptural quality which Jan van Eyck gave his figures. Instead of presenting the Magdalen full-face, as the Master of Flémalle presents his Virgin, Roger, like Jan van Eyck, shows her in three-quarter profile, to suggest a more three-dimensional form. However, what is uniquely Roger's is his emotional sensibility—and his resolve in conveying it; we are brought almost uncomfortably close to this woman's face. Neither charmingly coy, like the Mérode Virgin, nor majestically aloof, like the Autun Madonna, the Magdalen opens herself to us. Beneath her tight-fitting dress we see the roundness of breasts and belly, and in her eyes the anxious turning of a human spirit.

PETRUS CHRISTUS

Petrus Christus (ca. 1410–ca. 1473) was born in Baerle, near Ghent, in Flanders. Christus worked at various times in the towns of Cambrai and Bruges, where he evidently settled, and became a citizen in 1444. His rather small corpus of work—20 paintings in all—shows the range of his style, from an open, lyrical quality in his landscapes to a solemn introspectiveness in his sensitive portraits. Little is known of his training, but he seems to have been influenced at different times by Van Eyck, Van der Weyden, and Bouts. The flexibility of his technique and the emotional quality of his images make Christus a classic example of the Northern Renaissance approach to painting. He died in Bruges.

St. Eligius as a Goldsmith (1449)
By 1456 the art lovers of Italy had begun to sing the praises of Jan van Eyck and Roger van der Weyden, and while the artists of that country remained resistant to the northerners until some decades later, art in the rest of western Europe was now largely a reflection of the influence of Flemish painting. It was without question the art of Roger that foreigners most loved, and his popularity was tremendous at home as well as abroad. The artistic legacy of Jan van Eyck, on the other hand, was largely perpetuated by Petrus Christus. This task most likely fell to him by virtue of inheritance: it is generally believed that he took over Jan van Eyck's shop upon the master's death in 1441, and that he completed a number of works left incomplete at that time. As late as 1452, in fact, Petrus still permitted himself to make a copy after one of his great teacher's compositions. During that same decade, however, he also grappled with the very different stylistic ideas of Roger van der Weyden. This painting, which Petrus Christus signed and dated 1449, shows his mature reaction to both of his great predecessors. St. Eligius, the seventh-century evangelist to the Flemings and a goldsmith by trade, is seated in his workshop, weighing two wedding rings for the couple standing behind him. A bridal girdle is draped over the left side of the workbench. To the right, the shelves on the side wall carry the craftsman's glistening wears. To display these objects more clearly, the artist placed the wall at an acute angle to the workbench, which is parallel to the picture plane. This left an extremely restricted area for the figures to occupy, and tension is created by their necessarily tight grouping and closeness to the edge of their inhabitable space. Something of the same tension was provoked by Roger's close-up view of the Braque Magdalen. (See page 11.) However, no student of Jan van Eyck, who always placed his figures in comfortable spaces, could leave this tension unresolved, and to relieve it Petrus Christus cleverly propped a mirror up against the left corner. Here, in miniature, is a view of a wide, airy street, and of two casual passersby. The use of this device is entirely characteristic of Petrus Christus: he is thought to have been the first northern painter to discover how to use correct single-point perspective.

HANS MEMLING

Hans Memling (ca. 1435–1494) was born in Seligenstadt, Germany, but lived much of his life in Bruges, in Flanders. He was probably a pupil of Roger van der Weyden, and apparently was also familiar with the works of many of the major artists in the North at the time: Hugo van der Goes, Dirc Bouts, and perhaps Jan van Eyck. Memling's paintings are marked by graceful and elegant figures, fine descriptive detail, and a generally sweet tone. His complex religious works and his intimate portraits share a characteristic idealization of forms and images. Memling seems to have spent time in Brussels, probably prior to 1460; after 1465, numerous sources attest to his importance in the art world of Bruges. As the leading artistic figure in a prospering and influential city, he had an established reputation and received many commissions. Memling died in Bruges.

Virgin and Child with Six Female Saints (ca. 1475–1490)

In 1468 the people of Bruges, who could already boast of the preeminence of their city in European commerce, could also claim to have witnessed what may have been the social event of their times: the marriage of their dazzling and impetuous duke, Charles the Bold, to Margaret of York. Like a modern convention, the marriage sent profitable ripples throughout the Bruges economy as foreign guests indulged themselves in the city's numerous treasures. It was just about this time that Hans Memling was making his way to the top of the painters' hierarchy there, and he too may have been a benefactor of this lavish display. For most of the rest of his career Memling rode the crest of his city's prosperity: he died one of its wealthiest citizens. As this picture demonstrates, he was, like most of his contemporaries in the north, strongly influenced by Roger van der Weyden. In fact, it is almost certain that he was a student of that artist before coming to Bruges. In this work we see the Virgin and Child surrounded by six Virgin Martyrs, each of whom is identifiable by her own symbolic attribute. From the left they are St. Catherine, whose dress partially conceals the wheel; St. Agnes, caressing a lamb; St. Cecilia, the patroness of church music, with an organ; St. Lucy, the contents of whose bowl signifies the method of her demise; St. Margaret, with a dragon; and St. Barbara, who partially conceals her tower. Not reproduced here is a panel of matching size, which shows John the Baptist and a kneeling donor. In their elegant dress and their poised, articulate bearing, all of these ladies remind us of Roger's Magdalen. However, Mary, unlike her courtly companions, is uncrowned, and her hair falls directly on her shoulders; she commands our attention by her weightiness and the sobriety of her presence. Memling, it seems, would remind us that the absolute purity which she embodies neither has nor needs any material significance.

HIERONYMUS BOSCH

Hieronymus Bosch (ca. 1453–1516) was born in 's Hertogenbosch, in northern Brabant, and remained a resident of this town throughout his career. Bosch came from an artistic family, and undertook decorative works, altarpieces, and designs for stained glass as well as paintings. He was obsessed with the theme of the sinfulness of a hedonistic world, and his work is characterized by an unusual vision and a fantastic style. His paintings are teeming and chaotic fantasy worlds populated with nightmare creatures, arcane symbols and unusual allegories. Bosch was favored by King Phillip II of Spain and highly celebrated in his lifetime; his work gave rise to a plethora of imitators. On his death in 1516, he was referred to as *insignis pictor* (distinguished painter).

Ship of Fools (ca. 1495)
It is hard to imagine anything more different from the carefully practiced realism of Jan van Eyck or the delicate emotions of Roger van der Weyden than this motley image. Has its author, the remarkable Hieronymus Bosch, simply cast off tradition, to let it drift on the same strange seas that carry these misguided sailors? Who are these odd characters? What are they doing? Questions such as these cannot be answered easily in discussing Bosch. The one thing that is clear about this artist is that he was a startlingly individual personality, and his paintings are customarily filled with figures engaged in mysterious and obscure activities. What specifically do we see here? The shape of a small boat is easy enough to identify—how strange, then, that a wine bottle serves as its anchor, a spoon as its rudder and a full-grown tree as its mast. The crew of this vessel is, if possible, even less seaworthy. Leaving the more important chores of navigation to a naked figure who is actually outside the boat, they are led in song by a monk and a nun. The lookout position is held down by a drunken jester, and the ship's cook has scaled the mast to carve a fowl. These seem to be mere absurdities to us, but earlier observers saw them in another way. Writing in 1605, the Spanish historian Fra José de Sigüenza declared: "If there are any absurdities here, they are ours, not his; and to say it at once, they are a painted satire on the sins and ravings of man. The difference," he continued, "which, to my mind, exists between the pictures of this man [Bosch] and those of all others, is that they try to paint man as he is on the outside, while he alone had the audacity to paint him as he is on the inside...." (Stechow, *op. cit.*, pp. 22–23.)

ALBRECHT DURER

Albrecht Dürer (1471–1528), the son of a Hungarian goldsmith, was born in Nuremberg, Germany. Dürer is generally acknowledged to be the greatest of the German masters. His precocious talent for draftsmanship can be seen in a *Self Portrait* drawing made at the age of thirteen. In 1486, at the age of fifteen, he was apprenticed to the painter and engraver Michael Wolgemut. As a journeyman, in 1490, Dürer travelled to Colmar and then to Basel; in both cities, he worked with the brothers of Martin Schongauer. Shortly after his return to Nuremberg in 1494, Dürer embarked upon the first of several trips to Italy. After his return, he greatly increased his production of woodcuts, engravings, paintings, and drawings, and rapidly achieved both a great artistic reputation and widespread popularity. His work synthesizes the Gothic Mannerism of Schongauer with the influence of the Italian Renaissance. In 1520 Dürer began an extended tour of the Low Countries, where he was warmly received and where numerous honors were bestowed upon him. Upon his return to Germany in 1521, Dürer was largely occupied with religious speculation, having become a deeply committed Lutheran, and with the writing of several treatises on art and architecture. He died in Nuremberg.

Self Portrait (1498)

Before Dürer's time few independent self-portraits existed in the history of European art; during his lifetime they were more common, but none of his contemporaries, so far as we know, devoted as much time as he to recording his own features. For Dürer the self-portraits function primarily as straightforward declarations, pictorial equivalents of the inscription in the right corner of this painting, which reads: "1498/Das malt ich/nach meiner Gestalt/Ich war sex und zwanzig Jor alt/Albrecht Dürer" (I painted this according to my own features. I was twenty-six years old). In this self-portrait, furthermore, Dürer determined that every element of the work should reinforce that declarative function, either by direct support or by effective contrast. He defined the architectural background as two series of enframing, perpendicular lines, and his upright posture and crooked left arm fit neatly into this pattern. In the upper central portion of the painting he established a flat black background to act as a foil for the finely detailed treatment of the elaborately curled and glistening blond hair. In the curve of the arch he echoed the curving fall of the hat. He drew the horizon almost exactly at eye level, but otherwise contrasted the lyricism and color of the landscape with the carefully controlled interior environment, where he restrained the colors to a few shades of beige and grey. He also determined the role that the clothes were to play. Their colors, black, white, and brown, state in absolute terms the coloristic theme of the architectural background, while the stripes of the sleeve reinforce its compositional motif. Dürer's treatment of his features is also frankly declarative. It is impossible to detect any trace of a curve of the lips, or tension around the eyes, so that the expression of the face—indeed, the very essence of the man—is conveyed solely through the appearance of the features.

MATTHIAS GRUNEWALD

Little is known about the early life of Matthias Grünewald (ca. 1475-1528), whose given name was Mathis Gothardt Neithardt. He is thought to have been born around 1475 in Würzburg. Grünewald settled in Seligenstadt in 1501. In 1509 he entered the service of the Elector of Mainz, Archbishop Ulrich von Gemmingen, as court painter and architect; upon the Archbishop's death in 1514, he continued to serve his successor, Elector Albrecht von Brandenburg. However, as a result of religious persecution, Grünewald fled to Frankfurt in 1528, and subsequently to Halle. While he was familiar with the work of both Dürer and the Italian artists, and took from them a solid grounding in the scientific principles of anatomy and perspective, Grünewald rejected their Classical lyricism; his work was intensely expressionistic and Gothic in feeling. Grünewald died in Halle.

The Mocking of Christ (1503)

In sixteenth-century German art, Mathis Gothardt Neithardt, or Matthias Grünewald as he has been known since the seventeenth century, occupies a very different, but as equally important a position as Albrecht Dürer. Dürer, for his part, is credited with having been the most important link between the Italian Renaissance and the art of the north. Because he was so enormously prolific, his name was known to artists throughout Europe during his lifetime, and because his genius has such great breadth, his memory has been universally cherished since his death. Grünewald, however, made no overt attempts to assimilate the Italian style and instead brandishes an intensely personal vision of the world through a relatively small number of surviving works. He was only locally famous in his lifetime and was virtually forgotten after his death—his real name was only rediscovered in the 1920s. Nevertheless, the two artists are not so different as one might suppose after comparing this painting, one of Grünewald's earliest known works, with Dürer's Self Portrait. Grünewald, after all, chose as his subject one of the most torturous scenes from the New Testament: the mocking of Christ by the soldiers of Pilate. A woodcut by Dürer of the same subject shows that illustrations of the Passion—Christ's suffering from the last Supper to the Crucifixion—invariably called for a dramatic staging. But it was in this particular episode that Grünewald could best convey the dual themes of Christ's agonizing pain and its infliction on him by ordinary men. Grünewald himself pressed this point most fervently. Here the painter takes up a position only inches from Christ's crumpled, bleeding body, and hard by the green- and red-clad soldier whose figure flexes for the sake of the lash he is about to administer. Situated thus, he hears the inane whistling and banging of a musician in the background, and the undismayed mutterings of impious onlookers. These are recurring images in Grünewald's paintings: the nightmare of Christ's Passion was, to judge by his surviving works, the dominating image in his view of the world.

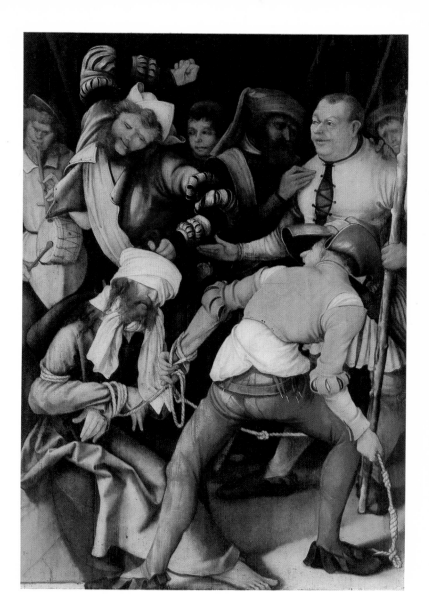

LUCAS CRANACH THE ELDER

Lucas Cranach the Elder (1472–1553) was born in Kronach, Germany. Along with Dürer, he is considered one of the two great masters of the German Renaissance. His earliest known work dates from 1500–1503, when he was in Vienna. In 1504, Cranach was called to Wittenberg by Elector Frederick the Wise and appointed the court painter. In 1519 he was elected to the Wittenberg city council, and he became Burgomaster in 1537. He continued to serve Frederick's successors, John the Constant and the Lutheran John Frederick the Magnificent, whom he followed into captivity in Augsburg in 1550, after John Frederick's defeat by the Catholic forces of Emperor Charles V at the battle of Mühlberg. While his treatments of mythological and historical subjects show audacious experimentation and flights of fantasy, Cranach also produced a large body of fashionable and flattering portraits of the upper classes. Particularly popular were a series of engravings of the great leaders of the Reformation. Cranach died in Weimar.

Portrait of a Lady (ca. 1530)

It has been observed that if Lucas Cranach had died in 1505 he might now be remembered as an even more explosive painter than Matthias Grünewald. Cranach, as a young man, had made a brief and apparently very successful siege of Vienna. There he poured out a series of passionate religious paintings and engravings and four insightful humanistic portraits, in which the sitters are set against breathtaking landscapes of the kind seen in the upper right corner of Dürer's *Self Portrait*. In 1504, however, Cranach made a decision which led to the most significant changes in his style. His portraiture, in particular, went from being the intricate exploration of mood and personality, to the calculated flattery of his courtly sitters exemplified by this painting, the portrait of an unknown woman. The most important element of this new style is the use of black background, though to describe this surrounding area as a background at all is to misrepresent its function in Cranach's portraiture. In his *Self Portrait*, as we recall, Dürer had laid in a similarly darkened area behind the head to serve as contrast for the fair skin and hair. However, if we compare it to Cranach's painting, we also sense the atmospheric qualities of the space represented by that area and the continuity of that space with the foreground. Nothing makes this more clear than the way we can see tiny slivers of this darkened area through the hairs which fall on the young Dürer's shoulders, and the way the same hairs reflect a light source in front. Cranach sought a different effect. His black, first of all, is utterly opaque and unmodulated, and cannot be understood to represent space. Secondly, this substance transforms the outline of the figure into an entirely closed, decorative silhouette. In fact, Cranach conceived the figure itself—to the woman's misfortune—in decorative terms: one could almost say that the subject of this painting is a dress. In departing so drastically from Dürer's style and from his own early style, Cranach departed from the mainstream of German painting; his only significant follower is his own son, Lucas Cranach the Younger. In so doing, however, he joined the ranks of the court artists of sixteenth-century Europe.

ALBRECHT ALTDORFER

Albrecht Altdorfer (ca. 1480–1538) was born in Regensburg, Bavaria. A painter, wood-engraver and limner, Altdorfer's work is noted for its excellent draftsmanship; he had the precision and keen attention to detail of a miniaturist. The first German artist to focus on landscape, Altdorfer produced innovative paintings in which the figures are overwhelmed by lush, idyllic, and exquisitely rendered forest settings. In addition to his artistic accomplishments, Altdorfer also achieved considerable prosperity and high civic standing; he owned two houses, was elected to the city council in 1519 and 1526, and was offered, but declined, an appointment as burgomaster. He died in Regensburg.

Landscape with Schloss Wörth on the Danube (ca. 1522)

This picture immediately distinguishes itself from all others reproduced in this book by containing no human figures. It is, in fact, one of the earliest independent landscape paintings in the history of European art. Long before Albrecht Altdorfer painted it, of course, artists of all eras made studies of nature in prints, drawings, watercolors, and architectural and decorative media. Additionally, landscape had always figured prominently in the backgrounds of early panel paintings, which can be seen clearly in the works of Jan van Eyck, Roger van der Weyden and Hans Memling. Among northern artists, Albrecht Dürer made the most extensive explorations of nature, and it was his example that inspired artists such as Altdorfer to venture into the previously unexplored realms of pure landscape painting. Lucas Cranach had been among the first to follow Dürer's lead, and, on the basis of his early paintings and prints, none of which, however, are pure landscapes, Cranach is known as one of the founders of the Danube School of German painters. These artists, though without a leader or a capital city, are united by an attachment to the dense forests and rolling hills of southern Germany, and by a bravado style reminiscent of the background of Dürer's *Self Portrait*. Altdorfer is their greatest and most adventurous representative. Born on the very banks of the Danube, he probably travelled downstream toward Vienna as early as 1511, and had known Dürer's prints since 1506. This painting, which is sometimes thought to be an imagined view, is closely related to a series of engravings that Altdorfer may have done around the same time. In both the prints and the painting our view is from a hilltop. The horizon is quite low, so that the extraordinary expanse which stretches out before us is telescoped into the lower third of the picture. Altdorfer organized this compacted view into a fore-, middle-, and background. The enframing pine trees demark the first division, the castle the limits of the second, and the blue-colored mountains the third. The winding road and the scallop-shaped river banks serve to reunite these elements. Similar organizational techniques had long been in use, but here nothing blocks the eye, and our view extends out and up into the crystalline air.

HANS HOLBEIN THE YOUNGER

Hans Holbein the Younger (ca. 1497–1543) was born in Augsburg. After receiving his initial training from his father, Hans Holbein the Elder, in 1514 he travelled to Basel with his brother Ambrosius to study with the painter Hans Herbster. Holbein achieved rapid success in Basel, receiving numerous commissions for book illustrations and portraits. After a trip to northern Italy in 1517, he became a member of Basel's painters' guild in 1519, and a citizen in 1520. Seeking to escape the mounting religious controversy in Basel, engendered by the Reformation, Holbein made a trip to England in 1526, where Erasmus recommended him to Sir Thomas More. He returned to Basel around 1528, but in 1532 he again went to England, this time to settle there. In England Holbein enjoyed the patronage of both the German merchant colony and the court, becoming court painter to King Henry VIII in 1536. His portraits from this period are remarkable for their artistic intensity and technical control; his subjects are rendered with a truly striking presence. Holbein died in London.

Anne of Cleves (1539)

Just as the preceding view of woodlands and sky will temporarily blind us to Albrecht Altdorfer's primarily religious concerns in painting, so this meeting with courtly gentility will momentarily obscure the fact that Hans Holbein the Younger had begun his career as a painter of religious subjects. In Holbein's Swiss homeland, however, the increasingly powerful Protestant church had forced painters to find other avenues for their talent. Holbein settled in London in 1532 but found the situation there much the same. Henry VIII's Act of Supremacy in 1534 was an ironically Luther-like gesture, and it opened the doors to Protestantism in England. Furthermore, its political impact on the King could have been disastrous, so, after the death of his third wife in 1437, he began a Europewide search for a bride to both bear him his long-desired male heir and to win favorable ties with some continental power. His preferred method of assessing the candidates was to send Holbein, his court portraitist since 1436. In the space of eighteen months Holbein made three trips abroad for the purpose of portraying a prospective queen. Two paintings resulted: the full-length portrait of the Duchess of Milan, made in 1538, and now in London, and this painting of Anne of Cleves, made in Duren in 1539. The image was painted on parchment, probably for the sake of portability; it would have been mounted on canvas in time for the wedding on January 20, 1540. A companion portrait of Henry, in Rome, was painted by Holbein for the same occasion. Christopher Mount, Henry's envoy and Holbein's travelling companion to Duren, reported his impression that the twenty-four-year-old Anne was pious, demure, and respectful of her elders, and, indeed, Holbein's likeness informs us that his subject was a hopeless ingénue. Holbein, perhaps anxious for an early settlement of these tiresome marital negotiations, seems to have tried to put, if not a good face, then a good dress on the matter. Her clothing has a strongly architectural symmetry. Henry and Anne were divorced on June 24, 1540.

JEAN CLOUET

Jean Clouet (1486–ca. 1540), also known as Jeanet or Janet, was a French painter of Flemish origin. Very little is known of his early life, and much of his work has been lost. Jean Clouet was chief painter in the court of Francis I of France from 1516 to 1541. While documentary records indicate that he produced religious paintings and tapestry cartoons as well as portraits, none of these works survive. Our knowledge of his art is based largely on a group of some 125 portrait drawings from this period; these intimate and expressive pieces are remarkable for their acuity of observed detail. Jean Clouet is thought to have died in Paris.

Portrait of Francis I (ca. 1525)

As in England, painting at the monarchic court of France entered the age of the Renaissance through the efforts of a foreigner. Like Hans Holbein, Jean Clouet arrived at the court of his royal patron to find that the royal portraits of the fifteenth century were, almost without exception, stiff and lifeless affairs, and a similar task of resurrecting court portraiture fell to both artists. Henry VIII saw in Holbein little more than a functionary, and indeed, Holbein's portraits of the King seem more concerned with conveying the power of the throne than the character of its occupant. Francis I, on the other hand, admired and valued his court painter greatly, as we know from a letter written by the King shortly after Clouet's death, and, as this painting shows, both King and painter were personally intrigued by the creative possibilities of royal portraiture. Instead of the dark, neutral background found in Holbein's royal portraiture, this King presents himself against an expanse of rich, red brocade. His costume is fabulously intricate, and provides endless fascination for the eye in its many ornamentations. These details are clearly ostentatious, but as our attention turns to the sitter's face, the King's expression foils us, for he is obviously unmoved by this finery. The lids droop and the manicured brows arch in faint bemusement, perhaps even boredom. Nor is there an identifying inscription, as in Holbein's portraits of Henry. We are expected to recognize this man, who flaunts his individuality, turning his head slightly to better show off the elegantly long nose and high bridge. The only overt reference to his office is the embroidered crown in the background. The mannered poise of both painter and sitter, which contrasts so strongly with Holbein's straightforward realism, makes us aware of how much more sympathetic Francis's court was to the Italian style than was the English court. On his death in 1541, François Clouet, Jean Clouet's son, succeeded to his father's post, and, in his paintings, the ties with sixteenth-century Italian art became even stronger.

NICHOLAS HILLIARD

Nicholas Hilliard (ca. 1547–1619), a miniaturist, was the leading English master of the Elizabethan era. He was born in Exeter, the son of a goldsmith. By 1562 Nicholas was himself apprenticed to a jeweler and goldsmith in London; his earliest portraits are thought to date from this period. By 1572 he was in the service of Queen Elizabeth as a limner and goldsmith, and in 1576 he travelled with her blessings to Paris. After his return, Hilliard retained his favored position at her court, and later became official court painter under James I, who granted him a twelve-year monopoly on court portraiture. His portraits are known for their meticulously painted detail, reflecting his early training as a goldsmith. Hilliard died in London.

Young Man Standing Among Roses (ca. 1588)

In the two decades that transpired between the death of Hans Holbein and the mature style of Nicholas Hilliard, leadership in British painting continued to lie in the hands of foreigners, mostly visiting Flemish and Netherlandish artists. Hilliard, therefore, became the first native-born British master to dominate not only the painting of his own country, but also to earn an international reputation. That his oeuvre consists almost entirely of portrait miniatures tells us a great deal about taste and patronage in Elizabethan and Jacobean times. Hilliard's miniatures, usually executed in watercolor on parchment and mounted on a card, are elegant, jewel-like objects made for an exclusively aristocratic clientele. Only occasionally are they full-length; generally they offer an intimate, finely detailed representation of the sitter's head and shoulders only. They are both formal, because of the careful attention that both painter and subject took to prepare a favorable image, and disarmingly penetrating, psychologically. In these respects they stand comparison with the portraits of Jean and François Clouet, which Hilliard may well have known. In fact, Hilliard was quite well informed about contemporary painting in Europe, and around 1600 he related both his knowledge of his profession, and his opinions of such colleagues as Holbein, Dürer, and Raphael, in *A Treatise Concerning the Art of Limning*. In this painting he follows his own counsel to observe nature scrupulously, to employ an immaculate technique, and to consummate perfect elegance of style. Across the upper edge of the oval runs an inscription, which reads *Dat poenas laudata fides* ("My praised faith procures my pain"; C. Winter, *Elizabethan Miniatures*, London, 1943, p. 26), a line from the writings of Lucan, the ancient historian. The phrase suggests a meaning that one might already have guessed: this suave courtier, hand held over heart and head pensively inclined, is pondering the questions of love. Love's joys are signified by the tiny white rosebuds seen against his cloak, its perils by the thorns which coil up around his long legs.

BIBLIOGRAPHY

Auerbach, E. *Nicholas Hilliard.* London: Routledge and Paul, 1961.

Baldass, L. *Jan van Eyck.* New York: Phaidon, 1952.

_____. *Hieronymous Bosch.* New York: Abrams, 1960.

Benesch, O. *The Art of the Renaissance in Northern Europe.* Cambridge: Harvard University Press, 1945.

_____. *German Painting from Dürer to Holbein.* Cleveland: Skira, 1966.

Blunt, A. *Art and Architecture in France, 1500–1700.* London and Baltimore: Penguin Books, 1954.

Cuttler, C.D. *Northern Painting.* New York: Rinehart and Winston, 1968.

Friedländer, M.J. *Lucas Cranach.* Berlin: Deutscher verein für Kunstwissenschaft, 1932.

_____. *Early Netherlandish Painting.* Leiden: A.W. Sijthoff, 1967.

Ganz, P. *The Paintings of Hans Holbein.* London: Phaidon, 1950.

Mellen, P. *Jean Clouet.* London: Phaidon, 1971.

Panofsky, E. *Early Netherlandish Painting, its Origins and Character.* Cambridge: Harvard University Press, 1953.

_____. *Life and Art of Albrecht Dürer.* Princeton: Princeton University Press, 1955.

Pevsner, N. and Meier, M. *Grünewald.* New York: Abrams, 1958.

Pope-Hennessy, J.W. *The Portrait in the Renaissance.* New York: Bollingen, 1966.

Schabacker, P. *Petrus Christus.* Utrecht: Haentjens Dekker and Gumbert, 1974.

Stechow, W. *Northern Renaissance Art 1400–1600, Sources and Documents.* Englewood Cliffs: Prentice Hall, 1966.

_____. *Pieter Bruegel the Elder.* New York: Abrams, 1969.

Voll, K. *The Work of Hans Memling.* New York: Brentano's, 1913.

Waterhouse, E.K. *Painting in Britain 1530–1790.* London and Baltimore: Penguin Books, 1953.

Winter, C. *Elizabethan Miniature.* London and New York: Penguin, 1943.

Winzinger, F. *Albrecht Altdorfer.* Munich: R. Piper, 1975.